LUFTWAFFE IN COLOUR
THE VICTORY YEARS 1939–1942

LUFTWAFFE IN COLOUR

The Victory Years 1939–1942

CHRISTOPHE CONY
& JEAN-LOUIS ROBA

CASEMATE | publishers
Philadelphia & Oxford

First published in the United States of America and Great Britain in 2016. Reprinted in 2017 by
CASEMATE PUBLISHERS
1950 Lawrence Road, Havertown, PA 19083, USA
and
The Old Music Hall, 106-108 Cowley Road, Oxford, OX4 1JE, UK

Paperback Edition: ISBN 978-1-61200-408-2
Digital Edition: ISBN 978-1-61200-410-5

A CIP record for this book is available from the Library of Congress and the British Library

Printed and bound by Replika Press Pvt Ltd, India

For a complete list of Casemate titles, please contact:

CASEMATE PUBLISHERS (US)
Telephone (610) 853-9131
Fax (610) 853-9146
Email: casemate@casematepublishers.com
www.casematepublishers.com

CASEMATE PUBLISHERS (UK)
Telephone (01865) 241249
Fax (01865) 794449
Email: casemate-uk@casematepublishers.co.uk
www.casematepublishers.co.uk

CONTENTS

INTRODUCTION

Eighty years after its creation, the Luftwaffe still holds a fascination that probably has no equal in the history of aviation. From almost nothing in 1935, this aerial force would prove entirely formidable by the outbreak of the Second World War. An offensive weapon par excellence, it would be the Third Reich's principal instrument of conquest during the Blitzkreig with such famous aircraft as the Ju 87 "Stuka" and the Messerschmitt Bf 109. When pressure intensified on all fronts from the end of 1942, it would continue to enjoy success, despite increasing reverses, thanks to the development of new combat tactics and revolutionary new technologies such as jet propulsion. Even in the spring of 1945 an Allied pilot flying over Germany still dreaded the prospect of an encounter with an Me 262.

Despite its immense prestige, there are relatively few colour shots of Luftwaffe aircraft and for one simple reason: the propaganda machine of the Third Reich reserved Germany's Agfachrome film process for its own official use unlike the US counterpart film process, Kodachrome, which was widely available during the war to both soldiers and civilians.

War correspondent Richter filming the pilot of a Fieseler "Storch" preparing to take off in May or June of 1940. The Fi 156 carries the factory code GA+WN.

As a result, the German soldier who loved photography had to be creative. A former pilot of JG 53 told us that when he was stationed in France in late 1940, he "raided" all the local photography shops in search of rare colour films. By including photographs from both magazines and newspapers of the time and also several private collectors, we have managed to assemble in this first volume over 300 colour photographs, many of which are previously unpublished, that trace the history of the Luftwaffe during the period of its greatest triumphs.

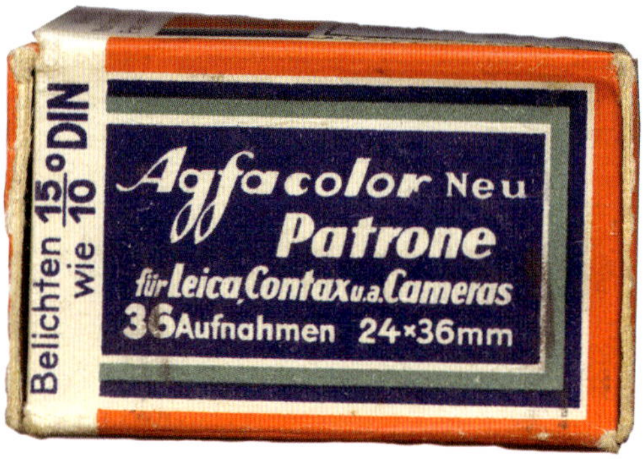

A box of Agfacolor Neu film.

The first efforts at colour photography date back to 1840 but the technology really developed in the 1930s. Leading early practitioners were the Lumière brothers with their Autochrome but their technique was complicated and used heavy glass plates which were fragile and very expensive. In 1935, the American company, Kodak, introduced Kodachrome, the first modern colour film. The following year, the German Agfa company launched Agfacolor whose integrated colour-sensitized emulsion layers greatly simplified the processing of films.

Colour photography was now available to the general public for the first time. However, the price of a colour film was significantly higher than that of black and white film and for this reason, as well as the difficulty of taking good colour photographs indoors, most photographs were still taken in black and white until the beginning of the 1950s. Thus the images in this book are extremely rare.

A Swiss advertising poster from 1937 for Agfa's Isochrom and Isopan black and white films.

Christophe Cony & Jean-Louis Roba

Part I

The Pre-War Period

Above: Gliding was a well-established national sport in Germany by the time the Nazi Party took power in 1933. Taking advantage of this enthusiasm for flight, the Third Reich did all it could to interest its young men in aviation by organizing huge glider competitions. This photo shows the famous Wasserkuppe peak in the Rhön mountains, which since 1920 had been the site of an annual gliding competition. This photograph of the 1939 competition which took place between July 23rd and August 6th is from *Signal* magazine. Various single-seater performance gliders can be seen including D-4-866, D-2-385, D-9,575, D7, 2193, D-12-454, D-7-331 and D-13-429 as well as the Akaflieg München Mü 13D. *(Signal)*

Left: FVA-13 "Olympia Jolle" D-12-411 at the Rhön Glider Competition in 1939. This glider was developed by Flugwissenchaftliche Vereiningung Aachen (Flight Research Association Aachen) for the 1940 Olympic Games in Finland, which for the first time would have included a gliding event, but the design was passed over by the Olympic Commission in favour of the DFS "Olympia Meise". *(Signal)*

Assembling a Göppingen Gö 3 "Minimoa". The cockpit is encased in moulded Plexiglas, a new innovation at the time. *(Signal)*

Above: Seen here gliding silently above the Rhön mountains, Gö 3 Minimoa D-10-921 was used in 1939 by the NSFK-Gr. 10 in Dortmund. *(Signal)*

Below: A DFS 108-68 "Weihe" just launched from the Wasserkuppe, displaying the markings of the NSFK-Gr. 14. The NSFK (Nationalsozialistisches Fliegerkorps) was an organization formed by the Nazi Party in October 1937 which brought together all civil aviation activities in Germany. This new paramilitary training organisation was much more politicized than its predecessor, the DLV (Deutscher Luftsportverband), created in March 1933. *(Signal)*

Above: Martin Schempp and Wolf Hirth under the wing of the 100th Minimoa built in their Göppingen workshop on June 30th, 1939. This model is the Gö 3 D-14-295, a glider from NSFK-Gr. 14 which operated in southern Bavaria. Note the metal airbrake installed behind the wing shaft.

Below: From January 1939, "D" (for Deutschland) was replaced by "WL" (for Wehrmacht Luftwaffe) on civil machines used in military aviation, such as this glider – Grunau "Baby" IIb – from the Münster Luftgaukommando, registration WL-VI-105.

From top:

A symbol of the rebirth of German aviation, the three-engined Junkers 52 was built before the war in many civil and military variants. This Ju 52/3m (W.Nr. 5797) was registered D-ATYZ in August 1937 to Lufthansa; it was named *Hans Hackmack* in honour of the chief pilot of the company, who was killed on February 26th, 1928 while testing the prototype of the single-engine Messerschmitt M20 transporter.

The Nazis put on huge displays of powered flight to attract the population to aviation. This two-seater Klemm L25e Vii R (W.Nr.836) D-EGUX of the NSFK participated in one such demonstration, the Tour of Germany (Deutschlandflug), in 1938, bearing the race number Z5b.

Also participating in Deutschlandflug 1938, this Ju W 34 hi, registration D-OMDO, is surrounded by many curious spectators who have come to see it take off from a small field in Marburg, a little over 70km north of Frankfurt.

The first production version of the famous "Stuka" dive bomber Ju 87 A-1 was still limited by its Junkers Jumo 210 Da engine, which only produced 680 hp. It could only carry a 250 kg bomb, or a 500 kg bomb if the pilot flew alone (without the rear gunner/observer).

Above: Amongst the new generation of modern machines developed by German engineers was this magnificent Bf 108 B-1 D-IOIO, built by Willy Messerschmitt, photographed above the Alps in about 1936. It was the direct precursor to the famous Bf 109, of which more were built than any other fighter aircraft in the history of aviation.

Below: Despite its outdated look, the Heinkel He 51 was the spearhead of the German fighters when the Luftwaffe was officially established on March 1st, 1935. By the time this photograph was taken in the late 1930s, this type of aircraft had been relegated to a training role only. This He 51B-1, W.Nr. 110 "Yellow 36", retained the blue engine cowling it had had in 1937 in I./JG 135, the future I./JG 51.

This advertisement appeared in a pre-war German magazine. The image at the top of the page shows the Hs 126 before its final assembly outside the manufacturer, Henschel Flugzeugwerke A.G., based in Berlin-Schönefeld; the aircraft shown are the Hs 126 W.Nr. 3109 to the left, and the Ju W 34 at the rear. The following two images were taken at Arado Flugzeugwerke G.m.b.H. at Güterfelde near Potsdam: left, the V-2a prototype of the Ar 79, D-EHCR (W.Nr. 2); below, the V-1a prototype, registration D-EKCX (W.Nr. 1).

In peacetime the "Auntie Ju" was used to transport a little of everything, even geese and pigs. This is a Ju 52/3m G4e, as indicated by the wide cargo door to the right. The five-character code (in use from June 1936) does not appear in full, but it is possible to deduce that this is the "I" aircraft of 2. *Staffel* of 2. *Gruppe*.

Top: A row of Dornier Do 17 E-1s of 5./KG 255 in a field in Leipheim, Bavaria, during the winter of 1938–1939. The twin-engine aircraft in the foreground was named *Drossel* (thrush). When II./KG 255 was re-designated III./KG 77 in May 1939, its insignia of a gentian flower was adopted by another bombing group, II./KG 51.

Above: A publicity poster for the Junkers Ju 86, a twin-engined aircraft used from 1936 as an airliner as well as a bomber. (DR)

Left: Advert for the Daimler-Benz DB 601 engine, here used on the Do 17 S (predecessor of the Do 215) but better known for its use on the Messerschmitt Bf 109 E.

Above: A Dornier Do 17 Z prototype, D-ASBE, taxiing down a grassy track in Karlsbad (now Karlovy Vary in the Czech Republic).

Below: The era of the fighter biplane ended in the mid-1930s when Messerschmitt released a new single-seat low-wing model: the Bf 109. The first unit of the Luftwaffe to consider this revolutionary aircraft was, in February 1937, II./JG 132 "Richthofen", which took ownership of these two Bf 109s one year later following an official ceremony at Jüterbog-Damm.

Left: From July 1936, the Third Reich supported the military coup that attempted to overthrow the Republic in Spain; engaging in this civil war was, for the Reich, a good way of testing out its new army. Also supported by Fascist Italy, the Spanish Nationalists ultimately triumphed over the Republicans on April 1st, 1939. This flagbearer from the Condor Legion poses – following the victory – in front of a Heinkel He 111 E, with a Ju 52/3m in the background.

Right: The Third Reich gave its victorious "volunteers" a triumphant return with a parade in Berlin on June 6th, 1939, in the presence of Adolf Hitler and the head of the Luftwaffe Herman Göring. Pictured here is the commander of the Condor Legion, Generalmajor Wolfram von Richthofen, cousin of the famous "Red Baron", who himself scored eight certified victories during the First World War. Germany was now ready for war.

Part II

From Poland to *Sitzkrieg*

This shark-faced Ju 87 B-1 was reputed to be the S2+AC of the commander of II./StG 77; if that was true, this Stuka bearing the code "White 10" on its landing gear fairings belonged to Hptm Clemens Graf von Schönborn-Wiesentheid. It was not, in any case, flown by the officer to whom it was originally allocated, Hptm Alfons Orthofer, assigned at that time to the headquarters of the 3rd Air Division – the group that he would take command of in August 1940. *(Signal)*

Opposite and overleaf: II./StG 77 prepare for war on the Breslau-Schöngarten base, now Wrocław Strachowice airport, Poland, in the summer of 1939. Many of the Stuka aircraft still bear their factory-issued codes, for example VK+FS for the "White 8". *(Signal)*

Above: Hptm von Schönborn-Wiesentheid describes a manoeuvre to his pilots. Promoted to *Kommandeur* of III./StG 2 on April 16th, 1940, then to *Kommodore* of the StG 77 the following May, von Schönborn-Wiesentheid was killed in a Fieseler Storch accident on August 30th, 1944, while serving in Sofia, Bulgaria. *(Signal)*

Below: The Dornier Do 17 E-1 3Z+GP of the 6./KG 77 – with its two convertible BMW VI 7.3 engines – during testing in 1939. It was with this already outdated model (it had entered into service two years earlier) that Kampfgeschwader 77 performed its entire campaign in Poland.

Even before the end of the Polish campaign, this Ju 52/3m picked up a family of German nationals for transport to the Reich. Of the 35 million inhabitants of Poland in the summer of 1939, only 23 million (less than 70%) were Poles. The remainder comprised various ethnic minorities, mainly Ukrainians, Belarusians and Jews; but among them 750,000 people, or 2%, were *Volksdeutsche*.

Above: The opposing air forces initially saw little action on the Western Front—hence the name *Sitzkrieg* ("sitting war") that the Germans gave to this so-called "phoney war". Only reconnaissance flights, such as the one this Do 17 P-1 7A+FM of 4.(F)/121 is about to make, forced the French and British to launch their fighters to intercept them. *(PK)*

Below: A Do 17 P-1 in flight. Its code has been censored, but we can see clearly why this aircraft was nicknamed "the flying pencil". *(Signal)*

Reconnaissance flights continued through the winter, despite bad weather. Here, a Do 17 P-1 from Aufklärungsgruppe 123 is being refuelled; the beginning of the unit code 4U is visible on the fuselage. *(PK)*

Previous page: It was "all quiet on the Western Front" (to quote Remarque) for the Luftwaffe too. Still, this game of cat-and-mouse allowed some fighter units to get themselves noticed, particularly JG 53 "Pik As" unit, to which this Bf 1909 E-1, seen here undergoing maintenance, belonged. *(PK)*

Top: This fighter pilot, here joking with a fellow falconry enthusiast, is often wrongly identified as Lt Richard Leppla of 3./JG 51. He is actually Lt Herbert Kunze of 2./JG 77, seen here at the beginning of 1940 in Odendorf in the cockpit of the Bf 109 E-1 "Red 11" named *Sepp*. *(Signal)*

Above: The Bf 109 E "Red 13" takes off from Bönninghardt in February or March 1940. The aircraft carries the laughing devil insignia of 2./JG 26. *(PK)*

Above: A four-engine Ju 90 V-10 (W.Nr. 0006) transporter, registered D-ASND Mecklenburg on behalf of Lufthansa in June 1939, received the code BG+GX on its incorporation into the Luftwaffe. Seen here in the winter of 1939–1940, it was destroyed on the ground in November 1943. At the time, it was J4+HH of LTS 290.

Below: Two Heinkel He 60 leave their base in northern Germany in early 1940. Retired from the front line at that time, this single-engine resumed service in 1941 due to a shortage of modern seaplanes. *(Signal)*

Above: The He 111 P 9K+KH of 1./KG 51 in snowy Memmingen during the winter of 1939–1940. Note the nationality markings and oversized codes on the fuselage, added in an attempt to avoid any possible misidentification.

Below: An "Emil" landing at a German aerodrome at the beginning of 1940. The aircraft still bears the dark camouflage used at the beginning of the war; this was composed of two shades of dark-green paint, which covered the aircraft's top and sides.

Left: Mechanics fill the wing reservoirs of a Heinkel He 111 P of II./KG 26 (5. *Staffel*, as indicated by the red nose cone). This unit was very active in April–May 1940 during Operation *Weserübung* – the occupation of Denmark and Norway. *(PK)*

Below: The dorsal machine gunner of Ju 52/3m G3E CF+IZ (W.Nr. 6885) poses for the camera. This aircraft belonged to the KGrzbV 106, which participated in the invasion of Denmark and Norway.

Above: Photographed in the cockpit of a He 111, a navigator verifies his aircraft's flight plan before a flight. *(Die Wehrmacht)*

Below: A Scandinavian fjord seen from the cockpit of a three-engined Ju 52/3m. *(PK)*

For the first time in Denmark and Norway, "Auntie Jus" were used in large numbers to transport German parachutists charged with capturing strategic points such as enemy airfields. As can be seen in these pictures, the *Fallschirmjäger* were also deployed as reinforcements for the mountain troops of General Eduard Dietl, who had just taken the port of Narvik. *(PK)*

Below: Having already proved itself efficient in Poland, the *Zerstörer* ("destroyer") Messerschmitt Bf 110 once more got itself noticed during *Weserübung* thanks to its range, which was far superior to that of the Bf 109. *(Jacques Moulin collection)*

A long-range Ju 87 R-1 of 2./StG 1 above a Norwegian fjord. Though southern and central Norway were occupied by German troops even before the invasion began, combat in the northern sector, concentrated around Narvik, which was retaken by the Allies on May 28th, only reached its conclusion on June 10th, 1940.

The elegant transoceanic Dornier Do 26 seaplane was developed before the war by Lufthansa for a Lisbon-New York route. Brought together in October 1939 within the Trans-Ozean *Staffel*, the Do 26 V-1 to V-5 seaplanes – including this one with an insignia under its cockpit – participated in the Norway campaign alongside KGrzbV 108; the four-engined aircraft were responsible for transporting vital men and materials over rugged Norwegian terrain. Clearly seen in this photograph are the MG 151 20mm cannon mounted on the front turret, and the ends of the propellers, which curiously are painted in blue, yellow and red.

A beautiful view of the top of the successor to the He 59 within the Luftwaffe's *Küstenfliegergruppen*: the Heinkel He 115, a seaplane used for reconnaissance, anti-shipping and minelaying missions. This multi-purpose twin-engined seaplane successfully took part in Operation *Weserübung*.

Part III

Blitzkrieg in the West

Above: Bf 109 Es of *Stab* I./JG 3 in the countryside at the beginning of May 1940. The rudders camouflaged up to mid-height are typical of this group at the end of the "phoney war". The aircraft on the left sports a repainted vertical stabiliser, complete with two swastikas.

Below: The crew members of this 3./KG 53 Heinkel He 111 H-1 equip themselves before leaving on a mission at the commencement of offensive operations in the West. Their bomber probably bears the code A1+CL.

Above: Close-up of the insignia of I./KG 53, a diving eagle holding a bomb in its talons. This aircraft was named *Ansbach* in honour of the Bavarian base at which the squadron was formed in May 1939.

Above right: Curiously, there are no known colour photographs of the famous Stuka from May–June 1940. This ground crewman passing in front of a Junkers Ju 87 B-1 with a 50 kg bomb on his shoulder was reportedly photographed on the Eastern Front in the summer of 1941, though it could just as easily have been one year earlier in France. The Stuka could carry four of these projectiles under its wings, as well as a 250 kg bomb under its fuselage.

Below: A rare colour image of a Henschel Hs 126 in flight during spring 1940. The code H1+FH on this aircraft, just visible on its dark fuselage, indicates that it is part of tactical reconnaissance *Staffel* 1.(H)/12. *(Jacques Moulin collection)*

Left: SC 50 (explosive) or SD 50 (fragmenting) bombs dropped by Stukas could be equipped with whistles, as seen here, to announce their presence to their victims. *(PK)*

Below: He 111 P 1G+BP of 6./KG 27 takes off from Delmenhorst, south-west of Bremen, for a flight over the Netherlands in early May 1940.

Bottom: This He 111, code 1G+KP, of 6./KG 27 landed on its belly after returning from a mission. Despite the success of *Fall Gelb* (the invasion of France, the Netherlands and Belgium), losses were heavy throughout the campaign.

Above: Mechanics cover the Jumo 211 A-1 engines of a He 111 H-1 of 3./KG 26 after a mission. The *Staffel's* emblem is visible on the cockpit: a sitting black lion, with the inscription *Vestigium Leonis* (The trace of the lion) above. From the beginning of 1940, the "Löwengeschwader" specialized in attacking maritime traffic in the North Sea. *(PK)*

Below: The pilot and navigator of a Junkers Ju 88 A-1. This twin-engined aircraft, capable of operating in a semi-dive, was the fastest of the Luftwaffe's bombers. *(PK)*

Above: The menacing "muzzle" of a II./ZG 76 Bf 110 C carefully camouflaged with foliage in the French countryside. It is easy to see why this unit was known as the *Haifischgruppe* (shark group).

Below: Bf 109 E "Black 3" of 2./JG 2 photographed at the beginning of the campaign in the West. The personal insignia on the cockpit is as yet unidentified. *(Jacques Moulin collection)*

Two views of Heinkel He 111 1G+BM of 4./KG 27, alone and in formation, in May–June 1940. The mechanics have painted caricatures of animals under the cockpit.

Perforated by the gunfire of British Hawker Hurricanes, He 111 P B3+BK (W.Nr. 2497) of 3./KG 54 had to make a wheels-up landing on the afternoon of May 19th, 1940 between Épinoy and Oisy-le-Verger, 15 km south of Douai.

Above: *Stab* II./KG 2 "Holzhammer" en route to the Netherlands in May 1940. These Do 17 Zs bear the codes U5+GC and U5+GM. *(PK)*

Left: Pilots of 6./JG 53 rest in a field in Charleville, where the second group of the "Pik As" (Ace of Spades) was based May 21st–29th, 1940.

If its speed of 450 km/h made the Ju 88 A-1 difficult to chase down, it did not render it immune to Allied fighters. This aircraft from the 6./LG 1, attacked by two Hurricanes of No. 151 Squadron RAF, was left "wallowing" on the beach of Nieuwpoort on May 29th, 1940; this photograph taken a few months later shows its wreckage torn apart by the tides.

Right: He 111P 1G+JP of 6./KG 27 en route to Bourges in June 1940.

Below right: Bf 108 "*Taifun*" (typhoon) bearing the code RF+AG, photographed in spring 1940, was an RLM Flugbereitschaft (Air Ministry Flight Readiness) aircraft. It was seriously damaged in the summer of 1941 when its engines failed on landing.

The insignia of I./JG 27 on the engine cowling of a Bf 109 E, photographed during the campaign in France. It shows that this group was linked to Africa long before becoming famous for its actions there in 1941-1942. The red nose cone shows that this is an aircraft of 2. *Staffel*. *(PK)*

Dornier Do 215 B-1 W.Nr. 0048 NO+TB shortly after its delivery in spring 1940. Assigned during the *Blitzkrieg* to Aufklärungsgruppe Ob.d.L., the reconnaissance group of the General Staff of the Luftwaffe, this aircraft was later damaged by Soviet anti-aircraft defences on August 18th, 1941, before being 75% destroyed on May 18th, 1943, following a forced landing at Étampes-Montdésir while serving with 2. Flieger-Division. *(PK)*

Bf 109 E-3 W.Nr. 1490 "Black chevron circle" of Oblt Werner Pichon Kalau vom Hofe of *Stab* I./JG 20, at the end of the campaign in France. Later upgraded E-7, this aircraft's career within tactical reconnaissance *Staffel* 4.(H)/12 came to an end as a result of an emergency landing on July 4th, 1942, near the Egyptian town of Sidi Barrani.

Part IV

The Battle of Britain and the Blitz

Above: A Messerschmitt Bf 110 C-4 of 8./ZG 26 flies over Caen in France in July 1940. Only just visible on its nose is the fox insignia of that *Staffel*. *(Jacques Moulin collection)*

Below: A profile shot of the same aircraft, 8./ZG 26 3U+CS. This was one of the first Bf 110s to be equipped with an armoured windscreen. Its pilot, an ace as confirmed by the six bars painted on the tail rudder, was probably Oblt Sophus Baagoe, who achieved his sixth "kill" on July 10th, 1940; it could also have been Oblt Karl-Heinz "Conny" Meyer, whose sixth kill came on August 18th, 1940. *(AVIONS collection)*

Stuka crews discuss a mission in front of a Ju 87 R-1 of 2./StG 1, whose raven emblem is visible on the cowling. Despite their reported successes against naval convoys crossing the Channel in July 1940, the Stukas suffered many losses in August, and were subsequently provisionally removed from operations. *(PK)*

Top: A red-coned 8./KG 51 Ju 88 A-1 refuelling at Étampes-Mondésir. The hatch to the cockpit is open. *(PK)*

Above: Two views of the Bf 110 C-1 3U+FM of 4./ZG 26 in early summer 1940. Recently transferred, it still bears the insignia of the III. *Gruppe* under the cockpit: a ladybird in a diamond.

Left: The 3U+FM during take off. The aircraft had been equipped with a rearview mirror on its windscreen, but the cockpit didn't have any interior or exterior shielding.

Above: This photograph may not be of the best quality, but it does show a very rare marking that doesn't conform to regulations: a triple chevron of a squadron commander on an Emil; the "correct" marking here would be a single chevron followed by two horizontal bars. This Bf 109 E-3 belonged to Obstlt Carl Vieck, commander of the JG 3 in July–August 1940. The staff of the wing was then stationed at Colembert, 15 km east of Boulogne-sur-Mer. *(PK)*

Below: Maintenance is carried out on a Heinkel He 111, the principal German bomber at the beginning of the Battle of Britain.

Above: An He 111 over the British coast. The gunner at the front is at his post, ready to open fire if the Royal Air Force appears.

Opposite: A pilot and navigator team in the narrow cabin of their Ju 88 A during the Battle of Britain. The red line across the cockpit windscreen indicates the angle for a dive attack. This shot is particularly interesting because it shows the sliding curtains for the crew to use to protect themselves from the sun.

Above: August 1940. Mechanics sunbathe in front of Bf 109 E-3 "Black 3" of 8./JG 53, probably close to La Villiaze on Guernsey in the Channel Islands. The *Staffel* personnel were ordered to hide their well-known Ace of Spades insignia with a 25 cm red band; their leader Oberstlt Hans-Jürgen von Cramon having fallen out of favour with the Luftwaffe. More than a month after he was replaced by Maj Günther von Maltzahn, the "Ace of Spades" ("Pik As") was reauthorized on November 20th, 1940. *(PK)*

Below: Bf 110 C-4 A2+AL of Hptm Heberhard Heinlein, *Staffelkapitän* of 6./ZG 2 from July 6th to August 16th 1940, along the cliffs of Cape Antifer near Étretat. After becoming commander of I./ZG 2, Heinlein was killed in an accident on September 28th, 1940. *(PK)*

Above: Lt Walter Blume of 7./JG 26 landed his overheating Bf 109 E-4 "White 13" at Calais-Marck after being hit in combat; a mechanic examines the damage to the engine. In the background is a Klemm 35. This shot was taken a little before Blume claimed his fifth and sixth aerial victories on August 15th and 16th respectively. The yellow markings on the wing tips and tail had just been introduced by Luftflotte 2.

Right: Repairs completed (damage to cowling can be seen in the foreground), the glycol tank of "White 13" is filled to return it to working order at Caffiers. Shot down in this same aircraft south-east of Canterbury just two days after his sixth victory, Blume returned to Germany gravely wounded. He returned to combat in 1943, claiming many kills over four-engined Allied planes with the I./JG 300 and I./JG 27 before retiring from service in June 1944.

On August 15th, 1940, a Spitfire Mk.IA AZ-H (N3277) *Dirty Dick* of No. 234 Squadron RAF was forced by Oblt Georg Claus of *Stab* III./JG 53 to land intact at the Cherbourg aerodrome. It was the seventh victory for Werner Mölders' former winger. Repainted with German markings, this Spitfire was then sent to Germany where it was extensively tested by the Rechlin *Erprobungsstelle* with the code 5+2.

Below: A Ju 88 A undergoing maintenance in summer 1940. *(PK)*

Briefing of II./ZG 2 crews at Guyancourt in early August 1940. The plane in the background is again the Bf 110 A2+AL of 6./ZG 2 *Staffelkapitän*, Hptm Heinlein (see page 56).

Above: During a visit to the German troops beside the English Channel in August 1940, Marshal Hermann Göring inspects a unit of Luftwaffe gunners. While there, he took the opportunity of casting an eye over England—through a rangefinder, of course. *(Signal)*

Below: A lucky 9./JG 26 pilot has managed to bring his Bf 109 E-1 "Yellow 6" (W.Nr. 2891) back to France despite being hit in combat at the end of August 1940. Note that beneath the fuselage is a fairing designed to protect a camera, which indicates that this aircraft was first produced as an E-5 reconnaissance craft and subsequently adapted into a fighter. Hit by a Spitfire south of London on September 30th of the same year, it was destroyed during an emergency landing at Caffiers.

Above: Bf 110s of *Stab* I./ZG 2 at Caen-Carpiquet in August 1940. Newer pale-bodied machines, such as Bf 110 C-4 3M+DB in the foreground, stand alongside aircraft still painted in the older and much darker camouflage. *(PK)*

Below: Messerschmitt Bf 110 Cs A2+IH and A2+BH of 4./ZG 2 in flight over France during the summer of 1940. These aircraft still bear the A2 code of their old unit, I./ZG 52, renamed II./ZG 2 on June 26th. *(PK)*

Left: A formation of Dornier Do 17 Zs on their way to Great Britain, photographed by a bomber or machine gunner. *(PK)*

Right: A Dornier Do 17 Z of 9./KG 76 during the Battle of Britain. The unit's insignia (three yellow runes on a red and white shield) symbolizes Tyr, the god of war in Germanic mythology.

Left: Junkers Ju 90 V-3 GF+GD (W.Nr. 4915), formerly D-AURE *Bayern* of Lufthansa, being refuelled at Bourges in September 1940. The large four-engined aircraft, which at this time had just been incorporated into the Luftwaffe, operated until March 1943 for the Franco-German Armistice Commission.

Above: This Erprobungsgruppe 210 mechanic carries on his shoulders a cartridge belt filled with 7.92 mm ammunition – approximately 1,000 cartridges in total. *(PK)*

Above right: Ordnance armourers load belts of 7.92 mm cartridges into the ammunition lockers of the four MG 17 machine guns of a Bf 110 D-0/B S9+FH of the 2./Erp.Gr. 210. This type of fighter-bomber was equipped with DB 601 N engines, which were more powerful than their "A" predecessors. By the foot of the man on the right we see the magazine of the rear MG 15 machine gun as well as the 20 mm drum of one of two MG FF M autocannons. *(PK)*

Right: Although only a *Gefreiter* (first class), this pilot being helped into his heavy fur-lined flying suit by a comrade is already the holder of the second class Iron Cross; he wears the silver badge, awarded to fighter pilots for flying 60 combat missions, over his left pocket. *(PK)*

September 1940: An officer of a heavy fighter unit listens to a report from one of his subordinates while ground crew carefully camouflage a Bf 110 at the edge of the field.

As the war in the air continued, the best fighter pilots began to keep tallies of their aerial encounters. Seen here at Campagne-lès-Guines in mid-October 1940, Oblt Hans Philipp (centre), *Kapitän* of 4./JG 54, stands with two *Leutnants* in front of his Bf 109 E "White 9", decorated with 18 "kill bars".

The mechanic of the Bf 109 E-4 W.Nr. 5057 "Yellow 1" was proud to be photographed with the score of its pilot, Oblt Josef Priller, *Kapitän* of 6./JG 51: 20 aerial victories and two planes destroyed on the ground. The last bar is red to symbolize the *Ritterkreuz* that Prill received on October 19th, 1940. This aircraft would at the beginning of 1941 become the mount of ace Herbert Ihlefeld, commander of the I.(J)/LG 2, before passing in 1942 to 15.(Kroat)/JG 52 on the Eastern Front. It would end its career in 1943 as a training aircraft of Jagdgruppe Süd of Marseille-Marignane.

Above: In October 1940, the catapult ship *Friesenland* left the port of Trondheim for Brest to launch its Do 26s for maritime reconnaissance missions along the British coast. Unfortunately, Do 26 V-5 P5+EH visible on board was lost during its first catapult launch on November 16th.

Right: Luftwaffe bombers also carried out night-time raids, like this Dornier Do 17 Z crew who are being strapped into their harnesses before leaving on a mission. *(PK)*

Below: Do 17 Z-2 F1+JT of 9./KG 76, photographed during autumn 1940, received a black wash on its underside for night raids.

In September 1940, the Luftwaffe began to seriously bomb London and other cities. This change in tactics also affected single-seat fighters, with the Luftwaffe converting a *Staffel* to a *Jabostaffel* in each of its fighter groups. In the JG 53 where these two photographs were taken, it was 3. 4. and 8. *Staffeln* that were re-equipped with E-1/B and E-4/Bs and began to operate in this role from the end of October 1940. The planes were equipped with an ETC 500 support that allowed them to carry one 250 kg bomb or four 50 kg bombs.

Two views of a Heinkel He 59 N of the 3./Seenotgruppe formed in November 1940 at Boulogne-sur-Mer from Seenotflug-Kommando 3. The insignia of the group, a gull holding a lifebelt, is clearly visible on the nose.

Left: Operating during the Battle of Britain from the small Dutch base of Schellingwoude, the He 115 seaplanes of 3./106 were engaged in setting mines along the British coast at night. Their undersides were painted black for these missions.

Above: Mardyck, autumn 1940. Mechanics adjust the MG 17s on "Yellow 10", a Bf 109 E of 6./JG 51. The aircraft bears on its cockpit the personal marking of its pilot, Oblt Walter Strengel, the *Segelfliegerabzeichen* (the glider pilot badge).

Below: Preheating the engines of a completely black KG 26 He 111 H in Norway. *(PK)*

Left: Abbeville-Drucat, at the beginning of 1941. Oblt Walter Horten (technical officer of Jagdgeschwader 26) poses in front of Bf 109 E-7/N "Double Chevron" of III./JG 26 commander, Hptm Gerhard Schöpfel, who won 21 victories. The gray camouflage on the plane is worth noting.

Above: On this He 111 H A1+LL of 3./KG 53, based at Lille-Nord in December 1940, even the national markings have been smeared with black paint, and only one letter, a yellow L, is left visible.

Right: Obst Adolf Galland, *Kommodore* of JG 26, welcomes a superior officer to Abbeville-Drucat in December 1940. The two Bf 109s visible in this shot are personalized aircraft: on the right E-4/N W.Nr 5819 decorated with 57 victory bars; on the left, E-7/N W.Nr. 5966.

Above left: He 59 N PY+NI (W.Nr. 2791) 2./*Seenotstaffel* at the port in Cherbourg in late 1940. *(Signal)*

Above right: Lt Herbert Schramm's Bf 109 "White 6" (7./JG 53) during take off at Le Touquet, November 1940. *(PK)*

Far left: Oblt Friedrich-Karl Müller, technical officer of *Stab* III./JG 53, photographed at Le Touquet in November 1940. He racked up 10 aerial victories, eight of which were taken during the campaign in France. *(PK)*

Left: A Jagdgeschwader 53 Emil in its protective bay at Le Touquet in November 1940. The "man in black" on the wing is an armourer of 7. *Staffel*, Obgefr Schnäbele. *(PK)*

Above: Hauptman Walter Oesau, commander of III./JG 3, leaning on Messerschmitt Bf 109 E-4 W.Nr. 1559 "Green 1" at Desvres in early 1941. This aircraft was previously flown by Hptm Wilhelm Balthasar, and still bears his "hit list": 27 aerial victories and 14 aircraft destroyed on the ground. Later changed to a Bf 109 E-7, it was destroyed in an accident on May 6th, 1942 near Darmstadt, whilst serving in 1./Ergänzungs-Jagdgruppe Süd. *(PK)*

Below: This Vickers Wellington Mk.IC LN-F (T2501) of No. 99 Squadron RAF was forced to land at an airfield occupied by KG 53 – probably Vitry-en-Artois – the night of December 4th–5th, 1940, during a raid on Düsseldorf. The twin-engined aircraft was repainted with Luftwaffe markings and transferred to the Rechlin *Erprobungsstelle* where it underwent testing with the code 5+4.

A Junkers Ju 88 A-5 of 9./KG 76 at Illesheim, Bavaria in early 1941. During the winter of 1940–1941, most Luftwaffe units returned to the Reich to rest and reequip. Having abandoned the idea of forcing Great Britain out of the war, Adolf Hitler had a new objective in mind: invade the Soviet Union.

On February 2nd, 1941, Sgt K. H. Jones of the No. 605 Squadron RAF was fighting several Bf 109 Es of I./LG 2 when he ran out of fuel and had to land his Hurricane Mk.IIA UP-M (Z2329) on the Coxyde (Koksijde) airfield in Belgium. The aircraft was quickly repainted with German markings and tested at Marquise by pilots of II./JG 51. Recoded DF+SC, it was tested at Rechlin before being used by I./*Jagdfliegerschule* 2 of Zerbst from August 1941 to May 1942.

An He 111 P of KG 27 flying over France in winter 1940–1941. The lower surfaces of the aircraft have been painted completely black.

Above: Mardyck, late April 1941. Obstlt Werner Mölders, *Kommodore* of JG 51, poses with mechanics in front of his Bf 109 F-2 "Double chevron and bars", with 65 victories recorded on the rudder. He was the top Luftwaffe ace, ahead of his friend and rival Adolf Galland.

Below: Bf 110 M8+CR of 7./ZG 76 at Stavanger-Sola in early spring 1941, a little before the "Shark Group" became II./SKG 210 and left for the new Eastern Front.

Part V

Marita and *Merkur*: Blitz in the Balkans

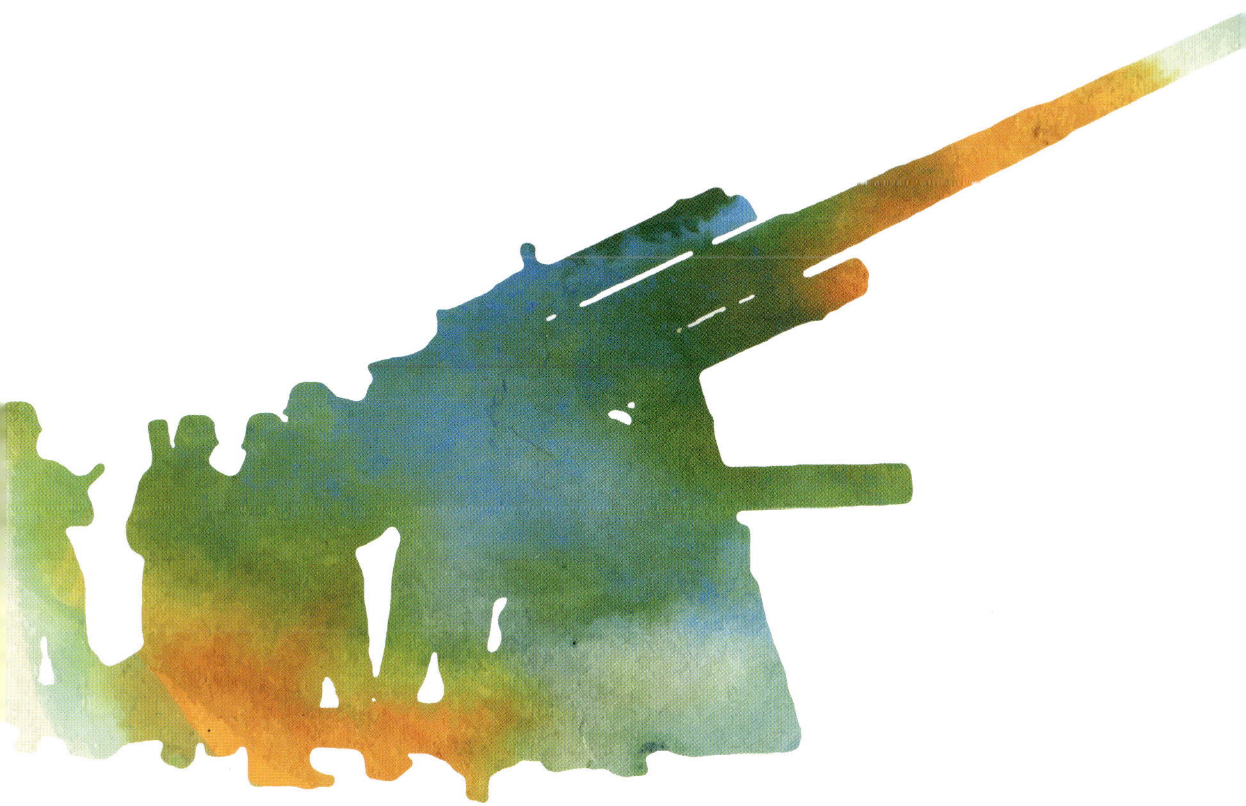

Top: Hitler had to delay his invasion of the Soviet Union by nearly two months, as he was forced to rush to the aid of his Italian ally Mussolini in the Balkans. A photographer present at Gorizia on March 5th, 1941 captured this Ju 87 R-2 arriving at Graz (Austria) to be delivered to the Regia Aeronautica. Though intended for the 208th of the 101st Squadriglia Gruppo, this plane would actually crash just after take off at Tirana, Albania. *(Giancarlo Garello collection)*

Above: In late March 1941, the Luftwaffe began to transfer a large number of units to the Balkans to prepare for Operation *Marita*: an attack on Yugoslavia and Greece. This field in Bulgaria was home to the Do 17 P-1 T6+HA of *Stab*/StG 2, as well as a Fieseler Storch and a Ju 52/3m. It is possible to make out in the background two old Dornier Do 11 bombers of the Royal Bulgarian Air Force.

Below: A Hs 126 in its protective bay, probably in Hungary a little before the beginning of Operation *Marita*. *(Private collection)*

Bottom: "Do you think we could win the war with oxen?" Crews benefited from some recreational time, even though the scope for tourism in Bulgaria was a little limited at the time.

A great view of a Ju 87 B-2 coded J stationed near Krésna gorge – which connected Sofia with Thessaloniki – in south-western Bulgaria at the beginning of April 1941. This picture was probably taken at Belica, where I./StG 3, *Stab* I. and *Stab* III./StG 2. were stationed.

Below: Two views of Bf 110 E-3 L2+SR of 7.(F)/LG 2 taken in early April 1941 at Sofia-Vrazhdebna. The yellow on the nose was carefully painted around the insignia of this reconnaissance squadron, a laughing devil.

Below: A yellow-nosed Ju 52/3m in Greece. On April 26th, 1941, the Auntie Jus played a prominent part in the airborne operation to conquer the Isthmus of Corinth.

This Ju 87 B-2, coded S7+DK, belonged to 2./StG 3 and was based at Belica, Bulgaria, in April 1941. All units engaged in the Balkan campaign received "high visibility" yellow markings to aid identification. *(PK)*

The enormous, though antiquated, four-engined Junkers G 38 transport GF+GG (W.Nr. 3302) *Generalfeldmarschall von Hindenburg*, previously D-2500 then D-APIS Lufthansa, seen during Operation *Marita*, which it took part in with KGrzbV 107. This plane was destroyed at Tatoi, during a raid by an RAF Wellington on the night of May 16th–17th, 1941.

Left: A 250 kg bomb is attached to a Bf 109 E-1/B of 6./JG 27. This version of the celebrated Emil had only four 7.7 mm machine guns. *(Philippe Ricco collection)*

Below: An 88 mm 36 anti-Flak cannon in the Balkans. The operators of this gun destroyed eight Allied aircraft.

Above: The Do 17 Z U5+DA of *Stab*/KG 2 in flight over the Aegean Sea during Operation *Marita*. *(Jacques Moulin collection)*

Top right: This Heinkel He 59 with yellow markings in spring 1941 is probably the DD+BB (W.Nr. 1990) of the 7./*Seenotstaffel*, a sea rescue *Staffel*. *(PK)*

Right: The Hs 126 B-1 5D+LK of 2.(H)/31 flies over a Greek town at the end of the campaign. *(PK)*

Above: Junkers Ju 52/3ms of KGrzbV 172 (at the bottom of the image) and Henschel Hs 126s of 4.(H)/22 (to the right) fly over Tatoi in May 1941. *(Private collection)*

Left: Heinrich "Heinz" Trettner, seen here as *Oberst* in 1943, was in 1941 the chief of operations in the general staff of XI. Fliegerkorps. It was in this capacity that he became one of those responsible for Operation *Merkur*: the invasion of Crete.

Below: A Bf 109 "Jabo" takes off in Greece. On May 22nd 1941, the Emils of JG 77 damaged the British ironclad HMS *Warspite*, which had already been attacked by Ju 88s of LG 1 and Do 17 of KG 2 a little earlier. *(Philippe Ricco collection)*

Left: Messerschmitt Bf 109 E "Black 7" of III./JG 77 at Belgrade-Semlin (Yugoslavia) in May 1941. The wing tips, trailing edges and a slim band on the fuselage are painted yellow.

Below: Loading fuel drums for Operation *Merkur* onto a Ju 52/3m G5E, whose yellow nose cones are just visible. This version is easily recognizable thanks to its small radio antenna and the extra window behind the cargo door. *(Jacques Moulin collection)*

Right: Two Ju 52/3m G3E aircraft of IV./KGzbV 1 operating in Greece in May 1941. The first military version of the 52/3m, the G3E has doors for passengers on both sides – a unique feature. Note 1Z+BF in the foreground has retained its pre-war three-colour camouflage, while the other has not. *(Jacques Moulin collection)*

Top: The Stukas of Stukageschwader 2 "Immelmann" constituted the spearhead of the Luftwaffe during their operations in Crete. In the foreground, Ju 87 B-2 T6+CK of 2./StG 2 still has sirens on its legs, a practice that had been more or less abandoned by this time. *(PK)*

Above: Mechanics of 7.(F)/LG 2 examine the damage sustained to the left rudder and wheel of a BF 110 C-5 L2+KR at Athens-Kalamaki, probably inflicted by Flak. This was not the first time that this aircraft had been hit; a red connector can be seen on the right rudder.

Left: Returning fron a reconnaissance mission over Crete in May 1941, a pilot of 7.(F)/LG 2 climbs out of his Bf 110 C-5 L2+OR at an airport in Athens-Kalamaki.

Above: Souvenir photo of Ju 52/3m 1Z+AY of IV.KGzbV 1. Despite substantial losses, nearly 500 Auntie Jus assisted the assault on Crete by dropping 10,000 paratroopers and launching 100 DFS 230 gliders over the island on May 20th, 1941. *(Private collection)*

Below: On May 19th, 1941, at Eleusis, DFS 230s were prepared for the airborne operation in Crete. The gliders bore no identification other than coloured bands on their fuselages, giving them the element of surprise on arrival at their destination.

Left: A BMW 132 engine is hoisted into the fuselage of a Ju 52/3m. Aside from transporting paratroopers to their drop-off locations, these three-engined Junkers executed the majority of air transport missions during the Balkans campaign. *(PK)*

Returning from the Balkans in June–July 1941, this very colourful Bf 110 C-4/B M8+AP of 6./ZG 76 was photographed on the ground at Magdeburg-Ost. It is seen here in the process of being transferred to another unit on the Eastern Front where new operations called for more German air forces.

Above: Having concluded Operation *Merkur* successfully, these members of the Luftwaffe in Crete relaxed by organizing a jousting tournament with donkeys as mounts.

Below: *Fallschirmjäger* parachuting from a Ju 52/3m at low altitude during a training exercise. *(Jacques Moulin collection)*

The fighter groups that left the Balkans at the end of April 1941 left their Messerschmitt Bf 109 Es behind to allow those who had participated in the assault on Crete to complete their missions. III./JG 77 acquired an Emil from Belgrade-Semlin that had previously belonged to II. and III./JG 54. This Bf 109 E-7 "Black 10" named *Lilo* was the old mount of Oblt Hubert Mütherich, *Staffelkapitän* of 5./JG 54, and retained his "hit list" on its tail: eight British and two Yugoslavian planes. The front section of the aircraft, which appears to have been taken from another aircraft, bears the cartoon bird of 8./JG 54 alongside the insignia of its new unit, III./JG 77 wolf's head. In the centre image, the "Black P" of II.(S)/LG 2 is visible in the background.

Part VI

Operation *Barbarossa*

This particular photograph is invariably found on the Internet along with the caption: *"Obfw Franz Dietrich Fadenau paints a new victory bar on his Bf 109 in 1942"*. However, F. D. Fadenau never actually existed. If the painter is indeed an Obfw pilot, a careful examination of the photo shows that the formation of the bars (seven "aerial" with the point at the top, five "on the ground" with the point at the bottom) is typical of only two groups: II. and III./JG 3. Six of their pilots reported four aerial victories in the West before completing their hit lists in the East in the summer of 1941. Only two of these were of the rank Obfw: Erwin Kortlepel of 4./JG 3 and Eberhard von Boremski of 9./JG 3. Since it is not the latter, the victorious painter is probably Obfw Kortlepel, who won his sixth and seventh successes on July 1st, 1941. He had 27 victories before the end of the year, when he was transferred to the Fl.Sonderkommando OKL, where he was injured three years later on December 16th. *(PK)*

Above: A Bf 109 F (probably of III./JG 54) is saluted by mechanics on its return from a successful mission. Most of the *Jagdgeschwadern* were reequipped with the "Friedrich" in early summer 1941; it completely outclassed the Soviet aircraft, so there was a huge increase in German fighter victories on the Eastern Front from June 22nd.

Below left: Oblt Heinz Lange in Dünaburg, Latvia in early summer 1931. On July 5th, he reported his fourth and fifth aerial victories. Though a pilot in 8./JG 54, he poses here in front of a vehicle marked with the emblem of I./JG 54: the coat of arms of the town of Nuremberg.

Below right: Hptm Franz von Werra (commander of I./JG 53) photographed in July 1941 in front of the wreck of an Ilyushin db-3 bomber. Shot down in England and captured the previous September, he escaped four months later from a prison train in Canada and made his way to the then neutral USA. *(Signal)*

Two years after the start of the war, the irreplaceable Ju 87 B-1 was still in use, as shown by S2+AP operating in the southern sector of the Russian front during the summer of 1941. This Stuka, named *Anton der Zweite* (Anton the Second), was that of Hptm Herbert Pabst, commander of 6./StG 77, with Fw Woletz as radio operator.

Above: Bf 110s of *Stab*/StG 1 in the central sector of the front in July or August 1941. Involved like the Ju 87s in assault missions, this unit marked the beginning of Operation *Barbarossa* by destroying several hundred Soviet planes and tanks on the ground, whilst also reporting large numbers of aerial victories.

Left: Three Bf 110 E2s of 1./SKG 210 over Smolensk at the start of the invasion. This version had air filters and deeper oil radiators. S9+EH (W.Nr. 4443) in the foreground and S9+GH (W.Nr. 4465) behind did not return from an attack on Wjasma on July 28th, 1941; as for the S9+FH (W.Nr. 4452) at the back, it was shot down near Pridnepowskaja a few days later on August 3rd.

Right: Another, later, view of the Bf 110 E-2 of SKG 210. Unlike the previous shot, in which the Messerschmitt bears the original insignia of the unit, formed in July 1940 as Erprobungsgruppe 210 (a map of England seen through a visor), the fighter-bombers are this time marked with the new emblem of the unit: a magnificent wasp.

A beautiful shot of an early version of Heinkel He 111 H in the countryside on the Eastern Front in 1941. Unfortunately, there are no details visible to allow identification of the unit it belonged to.

Top: The crew are helped out of Hs 126 6K+FL, a plane of 3.(H)/23 which has crash-landed in the Soviet countryside (maybe Owsischtschi) in summer 1941.

Above: Another Hs 126, the 6K+DL of 3.(H)/23 on the Eastern Front at the same time. The bright yellow markings of "tactical reconnaissance" are clearly visible.

Opposite top: An He 111 H-6 of KG 55 "Greif" drives through a Soviet aerodrome past mechanics bringing an SC-500 bomb to another aircraft.

Opposite centre: German and Romanian personnel celebrate the astonishing success of the first phase of Operation *Barbarossa*. But despite terrible losses, the Red Army was not defeated yet...

Opposite bottom: Photographed on the Eastern Front during summer 1941, the Ju 52/3m G5+HH belongs to the transport *Staffel* of V. Fliegerkorps, an aerial corps managed by GenFeldm Robert Ritter von Greim, and designated by a white "G" on its nose. This formation became, in April 1942, the Lw.Kdo.Ost, then one year later the transport *Staffel* of Luftflotte 6.

Above: Ju 88 A-5 9K+BB of *Stab* I./KG 51 photographed over the Ukraine in 1941.

Left: This Hs 126 is camouflaged by a makeshift shelter, representative of the often precarious conditions in which the Luftwaffe operated on the new front. *(Die Wehrmacht)*

Below: A Ju 88 A-4 of 1./KG 51 in flight at the end of summer 1941. Note that this aircraft bears its full code, 9K+GH, under its wings. *(Philippe Ricco collection)*

Members of KG 51 put on a small concert for their squadron, a group of Junkers Ju 88 crews operating in the southern sector of the Eastern Front in 1941. *(Bohumir Kudlicka collection)*

Left, from top:

A close-up of the insignia of the *Kampfgeschwader* 51 "Edelweiss" on the nose of a Ju 88 A-4. *(Bohumir Kudlicka collection)*

An Hs 123 A-1 carrying four 50 kg bombs under its wings. Though an outdated formula, this ground-attack biplane was so efficient that it was kept in service in 10.(Schl.)/LG 2 during the invasion of the Soviet Union. Hardy and reliable, the Henschel Hs 123s would only retire from the front in May 1944. DB+UC seen here already bears the badge of the assault infantry, but has not yet received a tactical code. *(Jacques Moulin collection)*

Mechanics adjust the shift mechanism of an enormous Junkers VS-11 propeller for an He 111 H-6. Unlike the VDM metal used on previous versions, the blades of this propeller are made of wood.

Right: Hptm Gordon Gollod, "boss" of the II./ JG 3, records his final mission during the summer of 1941. Later, as commander of the JG 77, he became the first pilot in history to achieve 150 aerial victories, claiming the 150th on August 29th, 1942.

Above: A pretty shot of Hs 126 H1+AK of 2.(H)/12 in the USSR. Behind it on the right is a Fieseler Fi 156 Storch, of which we can just see the first two letters of the *Stammkennzeichen*: PL. *(Peter Taghon collection)*

Below: A Bf 110 E of SKG 210 at Paderborn in August 1941, en route to the Eastern Front. The unit would be redesignated ZG 1 in January 1942; the first unit to bear that number was dissolved at the end of the campaign in France.

Above: Specialized equipment was not always available on the Eastern Front, so elbow grease was often needed to keep operations running. Here, armourers hoist a bomb into place under an He 111 H of KG 55 armed with a 20mm cannon in its nose.

Below: Again without appropriate equipment, these men are changing a propeller (with slender VDM metal blades) on a Ju 88 A-5 of II. or III./KG 1 in summer 1941. The dive brakes can be seen clearly under the wing.

Right: Two Ju 88 A-5s of 8./KG 1 prepare to take off in Pleskau in July–August 1941. In the background, V4+AS and in the foreground W.Nr. 4412 which would be damaged by Soviet anti-aircraft defences on August 25th near Rutschi. *(Philippe Ricco collection)*

Below: An anti-aircraft cannon defends a German aerodrome at Krivoy Rog during summer 1941. This is a Bofors 40 mm gun operated by a Hungarian unit.

A Bf 109 F-2 of 7./JG 54 photographed at the end of September 1941 in front of one of the hangars at the Siverskaya base. This Friedrich is probably the mount of Obfw Karl Kempf, who won his 27th and 28th victories on the 26th of that month.

The pilot of P2+HK (W.Nr. 3313) climbs into his aircraft, which a mechanic has just started up. This Hs 126 B-1 of tactical reconnaissance *Staffel* 2.(H)/21, seen on the Eastern Front in the autumn of 1941, is equipped with a winch (behind the fuselage), to tow a DFS 230 glider. It began *Barbarossa* in 9.(H)/LG 2, where it was damaged on the ground on July 14th at Moschki during a Soviet air attack.

A nurse comforts wounded men awaiting evacuation by air at the front in Leningrad in autumn 1941. In the background are several three-engined Ju 52/3ms, of which the first has the code 9P+IH.

Above: A Wehrmacht column photographed in the USSR from a Fieseler Storch in the winter of 1941-1942.

Below: Do 17 Zs of III./KG 3, identifiable by the code 5K painted on the fuselage, on a mission in the Moshaisk sector at the end of 1941, during the failed offensive by German forces on Moscow.

Above: The terrible Russian winter was a bitter surprise for the units of the Luftwaffe. Thanks to their strong gear, the Stuka could still continue operations, like here this Ju 87 B-1 which seems to belong to II./StG 1. *(Jacques Moulin collection)*

Below: A Friedrich of III./JG 53 in the Russian snow? Curious, as this group returned to Germany at the beginning of October 1941 to be reequipped before being transferred to the Mediterranean Front. The explanation is simple: when leaving, the unit left one of its Bf 109 F-2s at Konotop where III./JG 3 was then stationed, but they then left for Orel and didn't return until November, after the first snowfall. *(Jacques Moulin collection)*

Snow had also appeared at the south of the front. On Christmas Day 1941, Bf 110 E-3 L2+AR (W.Nr. 2437) of *Staffelkapitän* of 7./LG 2, Maj Paul Lube, had to make an emergency landing at Mariupol after having been damaged by Soviet anti-aircraft defences. *(Private collection)*

One of five Bf 110 E-3s (here the A5+AB) of *Stab*/StG 1 taxiing at Gostkino in February–March 1942. Its ETC 500/IXB fuselage rack has strangely been removed while its ETC 50 wing racks remain in place.

At the beginning of February 1942, the Soviet counter-offensive not only managed to reach Moscow, but also surrounded six German divisions in the pocket of Demyansk, about 300 km south-south-east of Leningrad. A Ju 52/3m airlift by the Luftwaffe ensured the successful resupply of 100,000 men trapped by the weather until spring allowed a ground offensive.

Bf 109 F-4s of II./JG 54, seen here at the beginning of 1942 at Siverskaya, participated in the protection of the pocket of Demyansk in March–April of that year. To avoid sinking into the fresh snow, doors on the undercarriage were removed. In the photo below, the Ju 52/3m RF+NA of the FlKpLnRgt 1 can been seen on the left.

To speed up replenishment, this pilot is filling his "Auntie Ju" with fuel himself The large radio-antenna shows that this aircraft is a Ju 52/3m G3E.

Above: The bombers also had to be repainted with winter camouflage schemes, like this 111 H-6 1G+FP of 6./KG 27 in flight over Leningrad in February–March 1942.

Left: In February 1942, Oblt Wilhelm Kaiser, *Adjutant* of III./StG 2, was decorated with the *Ritterkreuz* as reward for 125 successful combat missions at the controls of a Stuka.

Below: A Ju 88 A-5 escorted by two Bf 109 Fs. The caption of this substantially retouched propaganda card claimed these aircraft were operating on the Eastern Front, but the Junkers Ju 88 does not have defensive armaments and the Friedrichs are marked with an unusual blue tactical figure at the rear of the fuselage. *(Private collection)*

Right: A fantastic shot of Hptm Hans Philipp, henceforth *Kommandeur* of I./JG 54, posing with his mascot (a young fox) at Krasnogwardeisk on March 12th, 1942. The ace has just been awarded Crossed Swords on his *Ritterkreuz* (Knight's Cross), in recognition of his 82nd aerial victory.

Two views of a De Havilland DH 89 Dragon Rapide used as a transit aircraft by *Jagdgeschwader* 54 on the Eastern Front. Originally used by the Latvian postal service, this aircraft (YL-ABC or YL-ABD) was recovered by the USSR during the annexation of Latvia in June 1940 and "liberated" by the German advance in early summer 1941 at Riga.

Part VII

African Adventure and the Mediterranean Front

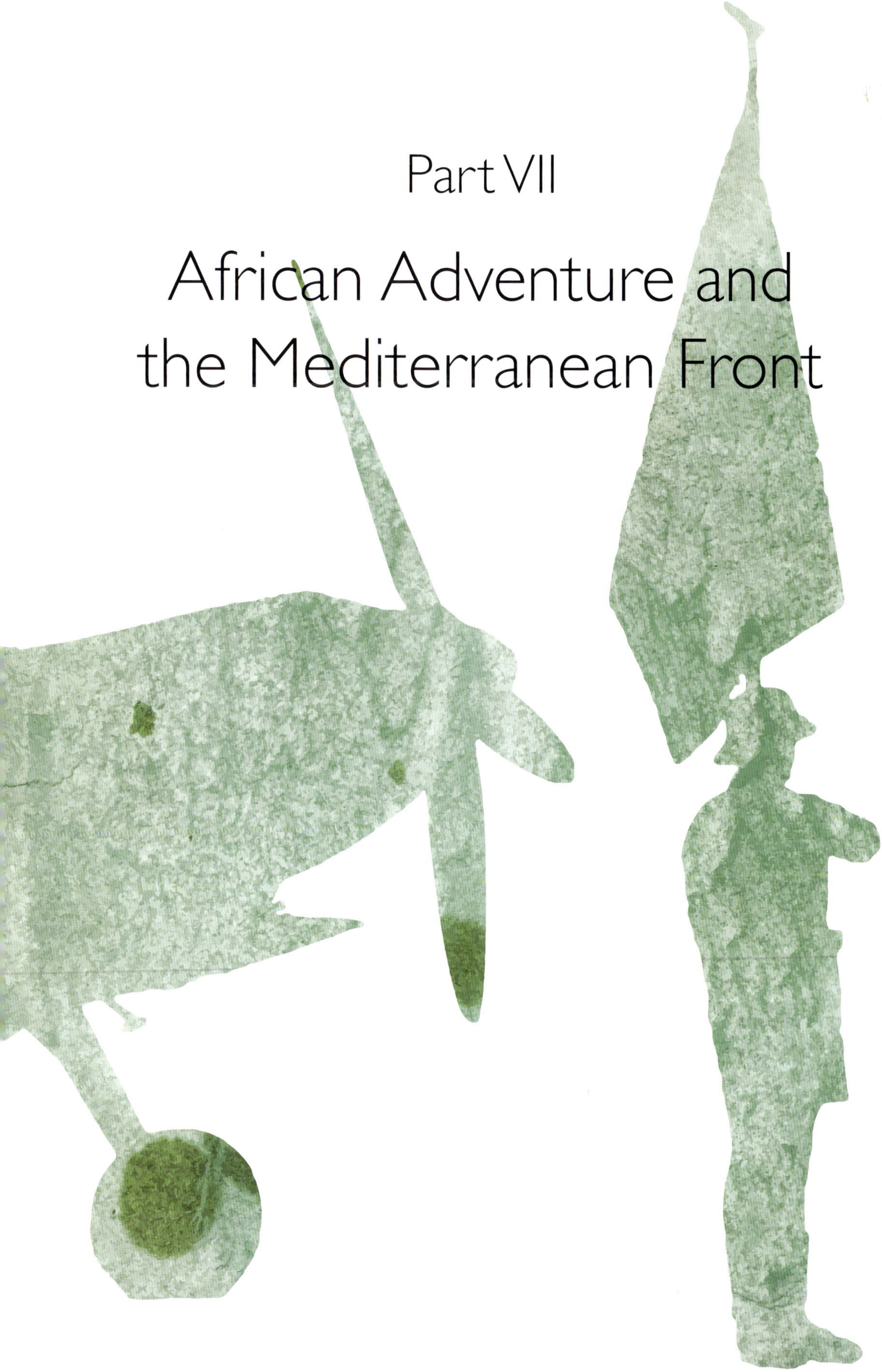

Top left: With the Italians also in difficulty in North Africa, Adolf Hitler decided in December 1940 to ensure the security of the African and Mediterranean theatres before engaging in the East. He sent the X. Fliegerkorps to Sicily, where they were charged with neutralizing the island of Malta and British maritime traffic between Gibraltar and Egypt. Among the units involved was Lehrgeschwader 1, whose Ju 88s were stationed in Catania.

Left: In February 1941, General Erwin Rommel landed at Tripoli to take command of an expeditionary corps, the *Afrika Korps*, which aimed to retake the territory lost by the Italians at the end of 1940. This Bf 110 E-2/N 3U+ED (W.Nr. 3890) of *Stab* III./ZG 26 still has its grey and green European camouflage.

Below: The Bf 110s of III./ZG 26 joined the operations at Trapani in January 1941. Here, a pilot of 7. *Staffel* proudly explains his aircraft to Italian Askaris.

Above: Photographed in March 1941 at Gerbini, Sicily, this is Ju 88 A-5 4D+DR (W.Nr. 3312) belonging to 7./KG 30, which has just arrived in the Mediterranean theatre of operations. The commander of this *Staffel*, Hptm Hans-Joachim Herrmann, distinguished himself on April 6th by destroying the cargo ship *Clan Frazer* in the port of Piraeus. The explosion sank ten other vessels and ravaged the port facilities. As for W.Nr. 3312, it was downed over the sea west of Crete by British anti-aircraft defences on April 21st.

Below left: Two Stuka groups, I./StG 1 and II./StG 2 on Ju 87 Rs, based at Bir Dufan, Tripolitania, in February 1941.

Below right: In 1943 "Hajo" Herrmann proposed the new "Wilde Sau" tactic for fighters. *(via J. Charita)*

Top left: Enjoying some free time, these Luftwaffe aviators visit the local markets in Libya.

Top right: Men of 8./ZG 26 relax beside a Bf 110 in the desert.

Above: Ju 87 R-1s of StG 3 in flight over the Mediterranean in spring 1941, at a time when the Stuka were accumulating successes at the expense of their maritime targets. The white bands on the leading edges of the tails of two of the aircraft are visible here.

Thanks to the paint stocks of their Italian allies, the Emils of I./JG 27 quickly received camouflage more suited to desert combat, as seen in these two photographs of "White 3" and "White 8" of 1. *Staffel*: upper surfaces were the colour of sand (*giallo mimetico*) spotted with olive green (*verde mimetico*), while lower surfaces and flanks were blue-grey (*grigio azzurro chiaro 1*).

Above: Despite having sent a small detachment to Sicily in March 1941, where it participated in many missions against Malta, I./JG 27 and its single-seat fighters only arrived at Ain-el-Gazala in Libya at the end of April. Seen here in May or June 1941, mechanics of 2./JG 27 play cards while waiting to prepare for their next mission. Behind them, Bf 109 E-7 "Black 3", an old I./JG 3 aircraft, still has its zebra-style European camouflage. *(AVIONS collection)*

Below: Due to the five white bars adorning the rudder, this Bf 110 D 3U+MR of 7./ZG 26 flying over Cyrenaica in spring 1941 is probably that of Obfw Franz Sander who won his fifth victory on April 3rd, 1941. A small (65-litre) supplementary fuel reservoir can be seen on the fuselage.

Left: Three-engined aircraft at Castel Benito, Libya, where their cargo is unloaded, while twin-engined escort aircraft (in the foreground, 3U+NS) are refuelled. The dust clouds raised by the aircraft gives an idea of the damage sand can do to engines that are not equipped with a special filter.

Right: Ju 52/3ms of KGzbV1 arrive in Africa escorted by the Bf 110 3U+NS of 8./ZG 26. This Messerschmitt was shot down by British anti-aircraft defence near Tobruk on May 2nd, 1941.

Above left: Ju 52/3ms at Trapani, Sicily. True workhorses of the Luftwaffe, these three-engined transport aircraft gave valuable services throughout the war.

Above right: Herbert Kuntz and his mascot, a lion cub. He is wearing a white summer cap, used between April 1st and September 30th. After distinguishing himself during the siege of Stalingrad on the Eastern Front in May 1942, this officer was decorated with the *Ritterkreuz* in March 1943.

Below: II./KG 26 arrived in Sicily in January 1941, then transferred to Greece where they remained until March 1942. Their He 111s, like this sand-coloured He 111 piloted by Lt Kuntz of 4. *Staffel*, bear the insignia of the "Löwengeschwader" with the motto *Vestigium Leonis*: the trace of the lion.

Standing to attention in Ain-el-Gazala, in the countryside about 50 km west of Tobruk at the end of summer 1941, a Luftwaffe flag-bearer stands in front of Bf 109 E-7 "Yellow 4" of 3./JG 27.

Above: Bf 109 E-7 "Black 8" of 2./JG 27 in flight off the Libyan coast in 1941. The usual pilot of this aircraft was Fw Franz Elles, who recorded his 4th victory (a Hurricane south of Bardia) on June 16th, 1941. He was captured in a Bf 109 F-4 on the following December 11th after claiming his fifth victory the day before. These two shots show the main characteristics of the "tropical" version of the Emil: the closure of the tail wheel cowling and the addition of a large sand filter on the intake.

Below: Lt Hans Remmer on his yellow-nosed Bf 109 E-7 of 1./JG 27, at Ain-el-Gazala during summer 1941. "Bubi" Remmer won his first victory on June 18th against a Brewster Buffalo of 805 Squadron of the Fleet Air Arm and his second on August 26th against a Hurricane, but he had to wait for the reequipping of his group onto Bf 109 Fs to become an ace in November.

Above: Returning to Germany at the end of July 1941 after a short tour on the Eastern Front, II./JG 27 reequipped with Bf 109 F-4s and two months later transferred to Ain-el-Gazala. Oblt Gustav Rödel is photographed here shortly after his arrival in front of his Friedrich, which no longer bears the white band of the Mediterranean theatre of operations. The formidable *Staffelkapitän* of 4./JG 27, already the holder of 21 victories, won 50 more before November 1942.

Below: Operators of a 37 mm anti-aircraft gun stationed on the perimeter of an African airfield. In its different versions (Flak 18, 36 and 37), this was the standard anti-aircraft gun to combat aircraft flying at low altitude.

Above: These two Bf 110 D-3/Ns or E-2/Ns escorting a convoy in the Mediterranean have supplementary 900-litre fuel reservoirs mounted under their wings. 3U+FT with yellow rudder flashes belonged to 9./ZG 26, while 3U+GS was an aircraft of 8. *Staffel* and bears its insignia on its nose: a white cockerel.

Left: The crew of a *Seenotstaffel* operating in the Mediterranean at the end of 1941 close the right engine cowling of their He 59 hydroplane before departing on a mission. *(PK)*

Below: Comiso aerodrome, in the south of Sicily, where a large part of Jagdgeschwader 53 was stationed from December 1941 to November 1942. *(Philippe Ricco collection)*

Above: Bf 110 C-7 3U+GS of 8./ZG 26, in flight over the Sicilian mountains, escorts a bomber formation on its way to attack Malta in early 1942.

Below: Hptm Joachim Helbig, commander of a Junkers Ju 88 of I./LG 1 in the Mediterranean, was the terror of the Royal Navy, who nicknamed the passage between Africa and Crete "Bomb Alley". He wears around his neck the Knight's Cross with Oak Leaves that he was awarded on January 16th, 1942.

Left: On February 23rd, 1942, Bf 109 F-4/Z "White 1" (W.Nr. 7452) of 10.(Jabo)/JG 53 crashed on take off from San Pietro. If the pilot was unharmed, the fighter-bomber certainly was not, and was classified 95% destroyed.

Right: Assigned to the Berlin-Staaken *Luftverkehrsgruppe*, the first Blohm und Voss six-engined seaplane – "Wiking" – served during autumn 1941 to protect the routes of the *Deutsche Afrika Korps* of General Erwin Rommel who was preparing to besiege Tobruk. BV 222 V-1 CC+EQ is seen here leaving Hamburg-Finkenwerder on September 10th, 1941. It arrived in Athens on the same day, and in Derna on the 15th.

Top left: Bf 109 F-4/Z "Yellow 2" of 6./JG 53 photographed in January 1942 at Comiso. *(PK)*

Top right: Ju 88 A-5 BL+ND (W.Nr. 3098), seen in North Africa in winter 1941-1942, was assigned to the *Flugbereitschaft* of Luftflotte 2, a VIP transportation unit. It bears its name, *Gert*, on its nose. This aircraft ended its career in 1943 in the Flugzeugführerschule C 6.

Above: "*With best wishes from 10.(Jabo)/Staffel*": Uffz Felix Sauer of 10.(Jabo)/JG 53 poses with a 250 kg bomb destined for Malta's defences in 1942.

Above: A *Rotte* (pair) from 7./ZG 26 over Sicily. 3U+HR in the foreground could be the aircraft of Obfw Helmut Haugk, who won his ninth aerial victory on December 8th, 1941, over Malta.

Below: Flying daily over the Mediterranean, the Ju 52/3ms were practically the only link with continental Europe – except the maritime convoys regularly attacked by the Royal Navy and Royal Air Force.

With its climate, landscapes and way of life, North Africa was something of a shock for the German aviators. Below, two officers admire a Libyan camel and its driver. Above, the same men examine a pair of Ju 87 R wings that have just been delivered from Germany.

A team on the ground prepare to mount a Rb 50/30 photographic device onto the fuselage of a Bf 110 E-3 of 2.(H)/14, at the beginning of 1942. With a full magazine of 64 metres of film, the Rb 50/30 weighed 72 kg. To improve its performance, the twin-engined aircraft carried no weapons; instead there are wooden tubes that simulate MG 17 machine guns on the nose and exit holes for MG FF guns have simply been drawn on with black paint. *(Private collection)*

Above: A close-up of a Luftwaffe Ju 87 R-2 being examined by Italian personnel in North Africa. *(Giancarlo Garello collection)*

Right: Hptm Helmut Naumann, of I./StG 3, was one of the leading Stuka aces on the African Front.

Below: Photographed in Casablanca in March 1942 in front of a French Douglas DB-7, this He 111 P-2 D-ARAJ (W.Nr. 2457) was an aircraft of Kontrollinspektion Afrika. Transferred to KGrzbV 23, it was damaged on January 26th at Konstantinovka during an airlift to resupply Stalingrad.

The air park at the Greek base of Skaramanga comprised Ar 196 A-2s of 2./125 as well as single-engined He 60s and twin-engined Fokker T.VIII Ws of SAGr 126, two coastal surveillance units. 2./125 were stationed from January to July 1942 at this coastal site in the Eleusis bay, 15 km from Athens.

An Ar 196 A-2 or A-3 of 2./125 on the Bay of Suda around 1942. The bows of the floats are painted red, the same as the propeller cone. On the right is a British cruiser, the HMS *York*, which was badly damaged by Italian speedboats on March 26th, 1941, was then finished off by the Luftwaffe while it was out of action.

Part VIII

In the West

Above: With the departure of the majority of Luftwaffe units from the Eastern Front, and more supporting the *Afrika Korps*, the defence of the Western Front and the Reich was left to a variety of fighter formations, such as 6./JG 53, whose pilots pose here with a Bf 109 F-4 at Westerland (on the island of Sylt, north of Germany) in July–August 1941. From left to right, front: Oblt Otto Böhner (*Staffelkapitän*), Fw Otto Göthe and Hptm Schönfeld (non-flyer); behind: Gefr Felix Sauer, Lt Helmuth Rose, Lt Hans Möller, Lt Dr Heiner Jörg and Fw Rudi Kranz.

Left: The *Staffelkapitän* of 6./JG 53 and his mascot in the cockpit of his Bf 109 F-4 "Yellow 1" in July 1941. Wounded in combat in Malta in early March 1942, Böhner was subsequently transferred to the general staff of the squadron as a ground-based technical officer. (*Geschwader-T.O.*)

Top: Maritime aviation, charged with coastal surveillance, benefited from substantial resources. This Arado Ar 196 A-3 (W.Nr. 0276) of Bordfl.Gr. 196 was photographed on the French coast in 1941; the seaplane still has its factory code DN+IF in white letters on its fuselage. *(PK)*

Above: The Arado Ar 196 A-2 T3+HK of 1./Bordfl.Gr. 196, probably at Wilhelmshaven in 1941. This unit provided equipment to the ships of the Kriegsmarine and also patrolled the coasts.

Right: An important element of life in the *Staffel*: the bar. The crew of 6./JG 53 painted theirs pink.

Above: A magnificent shot of the front of a Focke-Wulf FW 200 C-3 of I./KG 40 in 1941. This unit, specially reserved for long-distance maritime patrols, was based at Bordeaux-Mérignac from July 1940. *(PK)*

Left and opposite: Before their departure on a long patrol over the Atlantic, the crews of I./KG 40 gather around their group commander for a final briefing. The men are wearing their flight uniform: a K So/34 cotton jumpsuit with a Kapok-Schwimmveste Fl.30155 lifejacket. *(PK)*

An FW 200 C-3 at Bordeaux-Mérignac prepares for a mission over the Atlantic during the summer of 1941.

Crews head to their aircraft at Bordeaux-Mérignac in summer 1941. The five or six four-engined aircraft visible in this shot are the average number available in a unit, a suprisingly small number when one considers the results. *(PK)*

A "Condor" during take off. Having already sent nearly 800,000 tons to the bottom of the sea from June to December 1940, I./KG 40 achieved exceptional results during the first two months of 1941, sinking 37 ships. But increasing British defences soon slowed the pace of enemy; the unit claimed only 17 vessels from March until July, and only four more by the end of the year. *(PK)*

I./JG 52, responsible for protecting the Dutch coasts, used aircraft such as this Bf 109 F-2 "Black Chevron 4" (W.Nr. 8165) of the *Stab* photographed at Katwijk in September 1941. This curiously camouflaged aircraft would crash due to engine failure during take off on the 27th of the month, killing its pilot.

Below left: The insignia of I./JG 52, a giant hand grabbing a Spitfire.

Below right: Confronted by the "non-stop offensive" of the RAF, the aces of the Luftwaffe had an impressive list of successes. Obfw Josef Wurmheller of *Stab* II./JG 2 received the Knight's Cross on September 4th, 1941, after winning his 32nd victory; this shot shows him visiting the Messerschmitt factory during the autumn, shortly before he joined the Jagdfliegerschule 1 at Werneuchen as an instructor.

Fighter pilots play cards between missions over the English Channel during summer 1941. *(PK)*

Above: A great shot of a Bf 109 F-4 of 6./JG 53 in the grass at Bergen-aan-Zee in September 1941. Note the command post ingeniously disguised as a farm.

Below: A few weeks earlier, a new-generation fighter equipped with a powerful BMW 801 radial engine made its appearance: the Focke-Wulf FW 190. Seen here on the tarmac at the Focke-Wulf factory at Brême in June 1941, just before being introduced into the Luftwaffe, is the very first FW 190 A-1 of the series: the W.Nr. 001 SB+KA which would be delivered to the II./JG 26 the following month. This aircraft was damaged on landing at Abbeville on April 18th, 1942. *(Jacques Moulin collection)*

A Bf 110 D or E of II./NJG 3 photographed from a Ju 86 at Schleswig in 1941-1942. The aircraft bore the code D5 of the squadron in pale grey on its fuselage, as well as a II in Roman numerals next to the insignia of the night fighter, the *Englandblitz*.

It wasn't until summer 1940 that the Luftwaffe became night fighters worthy of the name, to face the intensification of night raids by Britain's Bomber Command. The first group of these *Nachtjagdgeschwader* was I./NJG 1, which included the three officers posing here at Venlo (in the Netherlands) in spring 1941. From left: Hptm Gerhard Hitgen, air traffic controller, Hptm Werner Streib, group commander and Lt Hans-Dieter Frank. The latter two became respected aces.

Above: Ju 88 A-5(F) T5+BU (W.Nr. 0776) of the *Wekusta* 1./ObdL, a weather reconnaissance *Staffel* based at Bad Zwischenahn at the end of 1941.

Two Friedrichs undergoing maintenance between missions over the English Channel at the beginning of 1942. The main feat of arms by the *Jagdwaffe* at that time took place on February 11th–12th; they successfully escorted the battle cruisers *Scharnhorst* and *Gneisenau*, as well as the heavy cruiser *Prinz Eugen*, during their transfer from Brest to Germany… right under the noses of the RAF. *(PK)*

A debriefing in II./JG 26 during spring 1942. The *Kommandeur* of the group, Hptm Joachim Müncheberg, acts out his last combat for Oblt Wilhelm-Ferdinand Galland (right), as Oblt Theodor Lindemann watches. "Wutz" Galland was the younger brother of celebrated ace Adolf Galland, thereafter *General der Jagdflieger*.

"Jochen" Müncheberg was justified in his apparent happiness: from March 13th to June 2nd, 1942, he increased his "hit list" from 63 to 81 victories. The ace wears around his neck his Knight's Cross with Oak Leaves that he was awarded on May 7th, 1941. *(PK)*

Part IX

The Second Line: Schools, Factories and Training

A Luftwaffe instructor explains the controls of a Bf 108 B-1 to some of his comrades; this Taifun has the blue livery characteristic of the civilian version produced by Messerschmitt before the war. Behind it on the left an old Albatros L 82 and an ex-Czechoslovakian Praga E 241 are just visible.

Two views of Bf 109 E-0s of Werneuchen Jagdfliegerschule 1 during winter 1939-1940. The "18" is the W.Nr. 1784, the "19" being pushed by mechanics is the W.Nr. 1787. These pre-production Emils had already provided good service; they show traces of dirt and old national marks that have subsequently been painted over.

Three views taken in June 1940 at the Schule/Flieger-Ausbildungs-Regiment 53, a basic training school based at Gutenfeld near Königsberg. Above, the Klemm Kl 32 GF+HO during take off...

...here, an old Heinkel He 46 bearing the code DC+FT...

...and finally, a Gotha Go 145 being prepared for take off by a trainee pilot of Sch./FAR 53.

Above: This postcard shows the He 115 C DC+GR (W.Nr. 2767), photographed departing on a test flight at the factory of its munfacturer, Heinkel Flugzeugwerke GmbH. Assigned to the 3./506, this seaplane, recoded S4+FK, was lost on a mine-laying mission in the North Sea on the night of August 1st–2nd, 1940.

Below: Though the Fieseler factory of Kassel could count on the success of its Bf 109 E-1, which it produced under licence at Heinkel in Rostock-Warnemünde, its He 100 D-0 aircraft were refused by the Luftwaffe. This was more for propaganda purposes than anything else, as they were not armed. The three *Industrieschutzstaffeln* were finally dissolved in late August 1940.

Following the example of the French *Armée de l'Air*, the Luftwaffe began patrols to defend their factories (*Industrieschutzstaffeln*) during the *Sitzkrieg*. From February 1940 the Focke-Wulf factory in Bremen used four twin-engined FW 187 A-0 fighters commanded by the engineer Kurt Tank, promoted to the rank of *Leutnant* for the occasion.

The FW 44 J CO+CG (W.Nr. 2396) photographed during an exercise in late summer 1940. This Stieglitz is brand new, having just been built by the firm CKD in Prague in July 1940.

Above: Not all colour photos from this time were perfect, but despite its poor quality, this image is nevertheless interesting as it shows the Bf 109 E-4/B CI+EJ (W.Nr. 3744) of the Rechlin *Erprobungsstelle*: at the beginning of September 1940 this aircraft tested the 300-litre detachable supplementary fuel tank.

Below: At the end of the 1930s, the aerodrome at Köthen (south of Dessau) became host to a school of radio operators, but more importantly it became the principal test site for Luftwaffe radio-guidance systems. This FW 58 C seen in October 1940 carries the code CX+HB and bears on its nose the insignia of the Luftnachrichten-Versuchs Regiment.

Below: Ln-Versuch-Rgt Köthen used various types of aircraft for their tests, including this Ju 86 G W.Nr. 451.

Above: Hptm Ortloff in the cockpit of one of the Ln-Versuch-Rgt Ju 86 Gs in October 1940.

Above: On October 10th, 1940, Bf 109 C-1 "White 18" (W.Nr. 1732) of 2./JFS 5 crashed during take off at Parndorf. Although the aircraft was torn in half, its pilot, Gefr Bernhard Gronek, was pulled free having suffered only minor injuries. *(Dénes Bernad collection)*

Below: This factory photograph of an He 111 undergoing a test flight was used for publicity purposes by the Heinkel company during the war.

Above and right: Two views of the Messerschmitt Bf 110 C and D of a second line unit in 1940 or 1941. Though a censor has covered one aircraft's markings, we know that the "Red 17" is actually coded VC+DR, not VC+DM as shown here. *(Jacques Moulin collection)*

Above: This view of an Ar 196 seaplane offers a few interesting details, in particular the support for the SC 50 bomb and the canopy. The bump on the fuselage, at the rear of the engine, is the fairing on a fixed 7.92 mm MG 17 machine gun. *(PK)*

Messerschmitt Bf 109 Ds at a fighter pilot school based in Germany in the winter of 1940-1941. The different shades of camouflage are worth noting, as is the bright pink colour used on the propeller cones.

In late 1940 most fighter squadrons organized an *Ergänzungsgruppe*, a replacement and training unit, which often only had two *Staffeln*; each of these had as their insignia a die showing the numbers of their squadron. Here we see the nose of the Erg.Gr./JG 26 "White 12", photographed passing through Rotterdam-Waalhaven in early summer 1941.

A factory photograph of the Junkers Ju 88 A-5 CB+OF (W.Nr. 0406), which in 1941 was assigned to 2.(F)/ObdL. It was in this squadron that it was twice damaged on the Eastern Front, in July and August 1941.

Dozens of Avia B-71 bombers, a version licensed from the Tupolev SB-2, were retrieved by Germany following the occupation of Czechoslovakia in March 1939; 111 others were also built for the Luftwaffe, who used them for training and for towing targets. These two shots show the Avia B-71A VG+BQ (W.Nr. 127) of Luftdienst-Teilkommando 2/12 from Mannheim-Sandhofen, with the nose of an old French Bloch 152 fighter facing it. *(Private collection)*

Above: The B-71B SE+FX (W.Nr. 216), an aircraft of Luftdienstkdo. 61 from Bad Zwischenahn in 1941-1942, has retained its original brown-and-grey camouflage; but the moving surfaces of the tail and the front of the engine cowlings have been repainted yellow to indicate the aircraft's new function.

Left: Trainee pilot Gerhard Ille, who became a fighter in 5./JG 2 in 1944, poses in front of the FW 44 Stieglitz BO+CC of FFS A/B 123 from Agram, near Zagreb, in summer 1941. This photo was taken in occupied Yugoslavia.

Below: Equipped with skis to enable it to operate on snowy surfaces, the Bücker Bü 131 D-2 BD+AQ (W.Nr. 4157) of FFS A/B 123 is making its way to Govizice in the winter of 1941-1942. Formerly of the FFS A/B 115, this aircraft was 60% damaged during an emergency landing on February 4th at Wels.

Lt Harald Freiherr von Arnim (in the centre, wearing sunglasses) surrounded by trainee pilots of Jagdfliegerschule 5 at Villacoublay in September 1941. An instructor at the beginning of the war, von Arnim fought in the Battle of Britain with 8./JG 2 before returning to 3./JFS 5 to give the trainee pilots the benefit of his experience.